PAPERCRAFT THERAPY

A step-by-step guide to creating beautiful objects

ELIZABETH MOAD

ARCTURUS

ARCTURUS

This edition published in 2016 by Arcturus Publishing Limited
26/27 Bickels Yard, 151–153 Bermondsey Street,
London SE1 3HA

ISBN: 978-1-78599-183-7
AD004919UK

Printed in China

CONTENTS

CREATIVITY AND RELAXATION

Relaxation means different things to different people: many of us relax by doing and making something, such as baking a cake, sewing or gardening. But for some of us the prospect of expressing creativity through crafts can be almost frightening. When we were younger, colouring and drawing may well have been part of our everyday lives – a way of expressing ourselves. As adults we may have lost this outlet for creativity, only returning to crafting as a means of relaxation at the end of a busy working day.

There is a proven link between relaxation and creativity. Relaxation allows our unconscious minds to reveal creative solutions which, if stressed, we might not be able to visualize. There is plenty of evidence to support this: our ancestors knew that creative acts (such as sewing and cooking) were not just important to life, they also provided us with 'down time' – a period of peace and reflection – at the end of the day. Today our lives are generally spent sitting at computers, living in cyberspace, so to come back to the physical world and 'make' something with our hands is a huge pleasure.

So we need to be calm in order to enjoy the creative process; but being creative also

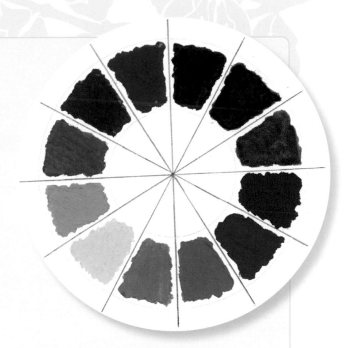

promotes relaxation. It is important not to fear mistakes, as the act of making an object should not add to our stress levels. As adults we often expect everything to be right first time and we are frustrated and angered by our errors. Artistic creativity allows us the freedom for things to go 'wrong', and it is often through making mistakes that the best results are achieved.

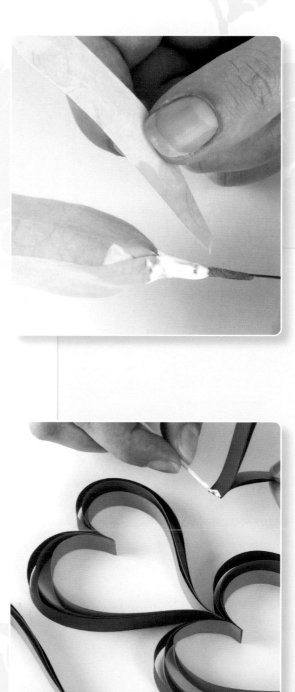

Where to start?

This book contains projects that will hopefully expand your creative horizons while at the same time allowing space for wonderful 'mistakes'! It is divided into two sections. The first includes quick and easy papercrafts to start you on your journey to relaxation and self-expression. The second section contains more advanced techniques. But you don't have to work through the book from start to finish; you can dip into and out of each chapter as you wish. Many of the projects can be adapted for the materials you have to hand or can purchase easily.

Get in the mindset and create a space

Start by creating a clear physical space in which to work. If you are at home, find an area that is quiet and calm. If you are using the kitchen table, declutter it to remove reminders of tasks to do. Switch off tablets and TVs and put phones on silent. You may like to have some soft background music playing, but it's important to try to craft without electronic distractions. Now clear your head; take a minute to breathe deeply and focus on the moment.

PAPERS

Paper is such a part of our daily lives that we tend to take it for granted and overlook the creative possibilities it holds. Plain and patterned papers have been crafted for centuries and are used both for practical and decorative purposes. It is important to select the colour and weight of paper most appropriate to your project carefully. Handmade papers with wonderful fibres, textures and patterns, and machine-made papers in a huge array of colours and designs are readily available online and from specialist craft shops. Papers printed on both sides are ideal for making decorations, such as the lavender box on page 68.

Grain

Just like wood, the grain of machine-made paper depends on how the fibres are arranged. Typically, they are parallel to one another across the sheet. Knowing the grain direction is important when tearing a sheet of paper. But not all paper has a grain – handmade paper has fibres that lie in all directions.

Weight

It's important to know which weight of paper or card to use. For example, paper may be too thin for a greetings card. It may need to be glued onto card so it stands up without curling. In Europe, weight is measured in grams per square metre (abbreviated to 'gsm' or 'g/m'). In the USA, paper weight is measured in pounds. General paper used in office printers and photocopiers is around 80gsm (54lb). A good average weight of card is 260–300gsm (176–203lb).

Plain paper and card is the most readily available, in all the colours of the rainbow. The standard size is 30cm- (12in-) square for sheets of card and patterned papers. An A4-size sheet is also a standard size in plain colours.

Patterned paper, such as wrapping paper (also called gift wrap) is generally sold in large sheets or on a roll. It is strong, available in a variety of patterns and very economical to use.

Textured paper, such as mulberry paper made from the mulberry tree, uses plant fibres to create a texture throughout. Its main characteristic is the random fibre pattern, which means that it has no grain, but is remarkably durable. Its unique texture makes it good for collage and other projects that can show its tactile characteristics.

Tissue paper is the lightest of all papers and is mainly used for gift wrapping to protect delicate items and make their presentation more special.

Upcycled and household papers, such as magazines, old books, music sheets, wrapping papers and old maps, are a great source for crafting. These papers are often lightweight and can be rolled or curled easily. With very old papers, be aware that they could be fragile and may tear easily.

BASIC TOOL KIT

The items shown on this page are your basic tool kit. Some specialist tools are also used in the projects, but it's best to purchase just the essentials initially and build up your kit over time.

A self-healing cutting mat is essential. When cut with a knife, the edges of the cut come together again, or heal, so as not to leave an indent. However, the mat will only cope with vertical cuts – angled cuts will gouge out areas. The printed lines on the mat can be used as guides for cutting, which saves time measuring. Mats also protect your work surface from glue and scissors.

A craft knife for cutting straight edges should always be used with a metal ruler on a cutting mat. Have a sharp blade in the knife and change it regularly.

A metal ruler is essential when cutting with a craft knife; a ruler with a cork base is best to avoid slipping.

An HB pencil and an eraser are required for marking lines and tracing templates.

Two pairs of scissors, one small, fine and pointed, the other larger, are useful for papercrafting.

A needle tool consists of a metal point on a handle; it is useful for rolling paper around and pricking holes.

A pair of fine-tipped tweezers is useful for picking up and positioning tiny items, such as gemstones.

Adhesive foam pads are great for achieving a raised effect when attaching items. They are adhesive on both sides – simply remove the backing paper and stick to your card or paper.

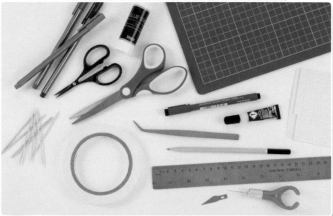

Cocktail sticks are used to apply small dots of glue to papers. Alternatively, you can use a needle tool to apply glue.

White PVA glue is ideal for crafting and gluing papers and card, but stronger glue is required to hold and secure items to metal or plastics. A glue stick is great if you just need a thin layer.

Double-sided tape is narrow and adhesive on both sides, and used for mounting paper or card.

Fine-tipped black pens are useful for doodling and drawing. Coloured felt-tip pens with a fine tip are a great addition to a crafting kit.

PROJECTS

1

Try the projects in the following section to get a feel
for the process of mindful papercrafting.

BOX OF SMILES

One of the easiest and quickest ways to boost your mood is to smile. Smiles do a lot more than let everyone know you're happy! A simple smile can reduce stress and help the body to relax. Smiling lifts the face, makes you look younger and helps you feel confident and more approachable. We automatically smile back at someone who is smiling at us, but try to smile even when you are alone! In this project, an empty matchbox is decorated inside and out with printed smiling faces. It is small enough to be portable or kept on a desk. It can be opened when you need cheering up; the bright warm colours will lift your mood.

You will need

❀ Empty matchbox, size 5cm (2in) wide x 8cm (3⅛in) long x 3cm (1¼in) deep
❀ Yellow and brown sheets of paper   ❀ Felt-tip pens in pink, orange and yellow
❀ Black fine-tip pen   ❀ Raffia   ❀ Glue   ❀ Scissors

STEP 1

Take a strip of yellow paper 6.5cm (2½in) wide x 28cm (11in) long and fold it at 4.5cm (1¾in) intervals along the strip. Fold it alternate ways to concertina the paper. Draw on circles of colour with the pink, orange and yellow pens. Do this all the way along the strip.

STEP 2

With a fine-tipped black pen, draw smiling faces on the circles and petal shapes around each one. Finally, draw light vertical lines for stalks.

STEP 3

With the orange pen, colour the box base. Wrap the outer case of the box with brown paper and use glue to secure it in place. If you wish, cut brown paper to fit inside the base, and secure with glue.

STEP 4

Wrap the box lid with a length of raffia. Cut a circle of yellow paper 3.5cm (1⅜in) in diameter and draw a smiling face on it. Thread a length of raffia through the circle and tie it to the box lid. Glue the folded yellow paper inside the box, then insert the box in the outer case.

Tip

Why not make boxes to give away to friends and family? Perhaps you could add messages or sayings inside.

WISHES AND WORRIES: PLANE

Most of us worry from time to time. Worrying can be helpful if it makes us take action. But sometimes the worry can overwhelm us, sapping our emotional energy. At this point, it's important to stop and look at what the worry is. Acknowledge and observe your anxious thoughts and feelings. If possible, send the worry away, at least temporarily. Here a classic paper plane is the vehicle for transporting your worry away. Make the plane and write your thoughts, worries and troubles onto it, then throw it. Even if you are just throwing it across the room into a wastepaper bin, it can be a visual metaphor for: 'I'm not going to worry about that now!'

You will need
❋ Sheet of A4 paper in a colour of your choice
❋ Pen

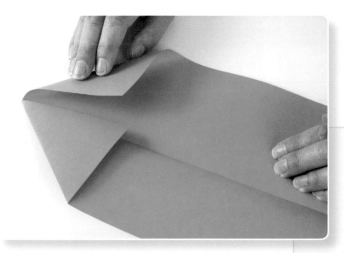

STEP 1
Take a sheet of standard A4 printer paper of any colour; I've used green here. Fold it in half lengthways, run your fingers along the crease, then open it out. Take one top corner and fold it down to the centre line. Crease this edge and then take the opposite corner and fold it to the centre line. Make good creases on these folds.

STEP 2
Now take one short edge and fold it over to meet the centre line. Press down and crease. Repeat on the other side.

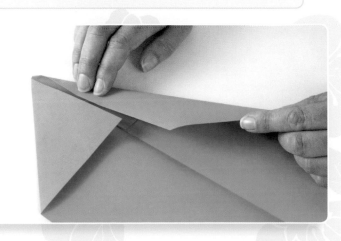

STEP 3

Fold the shape in half along the very first fold line you made. The two creased folds you made in step 2 should now meet each other and line up.

STEP 4

Finally, with the paper still folded in half, take the top edge and fold it back to meet the base. Turn the whole paper over and fold the other side to meet the base. You can either open out the paper and write your thoughts and worries on the inside or leave it folded and write on the outside.

Tip

Smaller planes can be made using smaller rectangles of paper.

WISHES AND WORRIES: BOAT

Let your imagination float away with your wishes on a paper boat. It is good to wish and dream; this positive thinking encourages hoping and believing. Wishes can come true, and maybe articulating them helps to make a plan of action. The process of crafting a paper boat allows the wish to be physically expressed rather than kept inside your head. You and your family could make some boats together; write your wishes on them and find a river to let them float away on. If you don't have a river nearby, line your boats up on the mantelpiece as a reminder to wish from time to time.

You will need

❀ Sheet of A4 paper in blue   ❀ Pen

STEP 1

Take the sheet of paper and fold it in half shortest edge to shortest edge. Crease the fold well. Now fold the paper in half again, and crease.

STEP 2

Open out the last fold you made. Take a corner and fold it over to meet the crease line down the centre of the paper. Repeat with the other corner.

STEP 3

Now take the bottom edge of the paper and fold it up towards the point of the triangle. Turn the paper over and fold the other side upwards. This makes a classic paper hat shape.

STEP 4

Take the shape and put your hand inside to push out the sides, then flatten it.

STEP 5

Fold the point of the top layer up. Turn the paper over and fold the other side upwards.

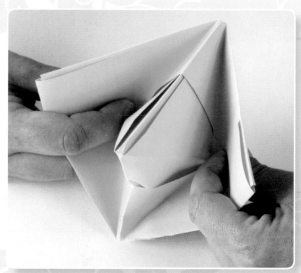

STEP 6

This is the tricky part: put your fingers inside the shape and pull outwards, moving the points apart. The boat shape will form if you squash the sides carefully. Write your messages on small pieces of paper and pop them into the boat.

Tip

These paper boats can be made in any size and any colour, using old maps, if you wish.

✂ ⋯⋯⋯⋯⋯⋯ **PROJECT 3**

TAKE HEART!

How about making a poster for your home? Put a smile on your face every time you leave the house by tearing off a paper heart and putting it in your handbag, pocket or using it as a bookmark. Why not cheer up the office notice board with this bright poster and spread love and happiness to your colleagues? You could include a message such as 'Take what you need', with tabs along the bottom with words such as Hope, Strength, Understanding, Peace, Love, Hugs, Happiness. . . . Or make a positive affirmation poster, with 'Today I will be . . .' as the main message across the top. Along the tabs write positive words such as : Amazing, Helpful, Polite, Happy, Strong, Calm, Relaxed, and so on.

You will need
❀ Sheet of orange A4 size card
❀ Sheet each of pink and red paper
❀ Ruler ❀ Black pen
❀ Scissors

STEP 1

Use a ruler and a black pen to make a row of dashed lines on the orange card 7cm (2¾in) up from a short edge. Then draw a series of dashed lines across to the short edge at about 3cm (1¼in) intervals, making seven sections.

Tip

This poster has seven tear-off tabs for the days of the week, but you could have five tabs for working days at your job, college or school.

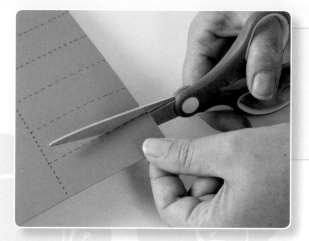

STEP 2

Take a pair of large scissors and cut along the vertical dashed lines. This creates seven flaps, or tabs, still attached to the main poster.

STEP 3

From the pink and red paper, cut seven small hearts using the templates on page 92. Glue one onto each tab. Then cut one large heart, two medium heart shapes and four smaller hearts. Glue these to the poster above the tabs. You can write on the central one: 'Take heart!'.

Tip

You could add smiling faces to the hearts with a fine-tipped black pen.

✂ ···

PROJECT 4

···

TREE OF LIFE

A powerful symbol of strength and growth, a tree has roots that reach down into the earth and establish a stable base. It grows and branches out, reaching new heights, then produces fruit or seeds as part of regeneration and continuation. Trees also provide shelter and protection – how many of us have sheltered under a tree during a downpour? And, of course, trees arc used to make paper. This simple paper-cut tree on a greetings card can be used to convey many messages to the recipient. We tend to send cards for happy or sad occasions, but it is also good to send one out of the blue to say 'stay strong' or 'branch out'.

You will need
❀ Two sheets of square, 13cm (5in) card – one blue, one brown
❀ Light and dark patterned paper in green
❀ White card, 13.5cm (5¼in) square ❀ Scissors ❀ Glue
❀ Cocktail stick ❀ Double-sided tape

STEP 1
Take the light patterned paper and, using small scissors, cut some leaf shapes. You can make a leaf with just two cuts of the scissors – don't worry about different sizes. Now cut leaves from the dark patterned paper.

STEP 2
Cut a tree trunk from brown card, using the template on page 92, and glue it onto the blue card square.

STEP 3

Using a cocktail stick, spread a small amount of glue onto each leaf and stick it to the card. Arrange the leaves with an even distribution of dark and light patterning. Mount the blue card onto the white card using double-sided tape. Add a message if you wish.

Tip

Any colour combination of paper works well for this tree design; even pages of an old book can be very effective as leaves.

✂ ······································

PROJECT 5

GRATITUDE JAR

We may often take for granted what we have and focus instead on what we don't have. It is important to remember the positive things in our lives, to think about the things we appreciate and care for. So how about filling a gratitude jar with mini-envelopes listing the things you should be grateful for? Keep a stack of blank notes near the jar so you can add to your blessings over time. Occasionally take out and read some of your notes. This can counteract negative thoughts when you are feeling down.

You will need

❀ Glass jar, tinted blue, 18cm (7in) tall

❀ Several sheets of A4 paper in mauve and purple

❀ Strips of pink paper 1cm (⅜in) wide and 12cm (4¾in) long

❀ Pen ❀ Twine, ribbon and a brown label

STEP 1

Cut the sheet of mauve paper into strips about 5cm (2in) wide x 10cm (4in) long. Fold twice to create a square of about 5cm (2in). Inside each piece, write something you are grateful for that makes you happy, such as good health, kind friends, a loving partner, smiles from your children . . . even the smell of fresh coffee!

STEP 2

Now take a strip of pink paper, wrap it round the folded piece of mauve paper and glue in place to seal your message.

STEP 3

Fill the jar with your pieces of paper. The whole family can be involved if you like. Make a tag by gluing mauve and purple paper shapes to a brown label. Tie it to the jar with twine. Write the date and 'Gratitude Jar' on the label. You could also make an accompanying 'positive affirmation' jar. Do this by writing confidence-building self-help messages, such as: 'I am creative', 'I am kind', 'I am helpful', 'I am thoughtful' on cream paper.

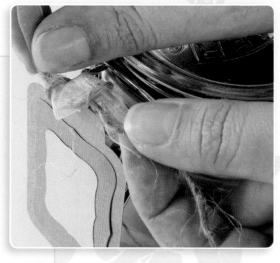

Tip

Use a jar you can get your hand into and out of easily. It is best to use a clear or lightly tinted jar, so that you can see the messages of positivity and gratitude.

BUTTERFLY FREEDOM GARLAND

Sometimes we get stuck in our lives, refusing to believe that wonderful things may happen in the future. Butterflies go through several stages in their lives before emerging in all their glory. Their transition has become a symbol for the life cycle. We can relate to these butterfly stages, as sometimes we withdraw into our 'cocoons' and at other times we feel triumphant, as if we have emerged into the light. Making paper butterflies can remind us that we are part of a bigger cycle of life. I've made a quick and simple garland from an old book, for a vintage feel.

You will need
❀ Gold-coloured 20-gauge wire
❀ Pages from an old book, cut into squares and ovals ❀ Purple organza ribbon ❀ Pliers ❀ Glue

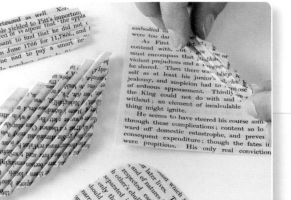

STEP 1

Take a 10cm (4in) square of paper and concertina it, starting at a corner point and folding across the paper. Make the folds as small and as even as you can. Do the same with an oval piece of paper, 6.5cm (2½in) x 9cm (3½in), starting at the longest edge and folding across the paper.

Tip

You can glue these butterflies onto a gift bag.

STEP 2

Fold both pieces of paper in half and glue them together at the centre. The square paper shape makes the top and the oval shape the bottom wings.

STEP 3

Tie a 15cm (5⅞in) length of purple organza ribbon in a knot around the centre. Arrange the ends of the ribbon so that they resemble antennae.

STEP 4

Now pull some of the concertina folds out gently to create a butterfly wing shape.

STEP 5

Thread a length of gold wire through the ribbon of each butterfly to make a garland. If you don't have wire, attach the butterflies to a length of strong ribbon. Make as many butterflies as you wish. You can make them in a range of sizes and colours.

✂ PROJECT 7

BIRD OF PEACE

The dove is a beautiful, calm image, evoking feelings of tranquillity and relaxation. It is often used at Christmas time as a symbol of peace, but could also be sent to make amends following a family argument. Not all families are harmonious and there are often bumpy moments where feelings are hurt and offence is taken. Discord among family and friends is disturbing and unsettling because we depend on them for love and support. Why not make a simple dove card to send out to heal a rift?

You will need
❋ Dark blue card, folded in half to make a 13cm (5in) square ❋ Pencil
❋ Small piece of green card
❋ Light blue paper ❋ Small foam pads
❋ Dark blue fine-tipped pen
❋ Small scissors

STEP 1
Using the templates on page 93, draw round each shape on light blue paper in pencil. Cut the two shapes out with small scissors.

STEP 2
With the dark blue pen, mark an eye on the dove. Cut an olive branch from green card, using the template on page 93. Glue the branch to the beak of the dove.

STEP 3

Glue the single wing directly onto the dark blue folded card. Then apply small foam pads to the reverse of the dove and mount it over the wing on the card. Add a message inside the card if you wish.

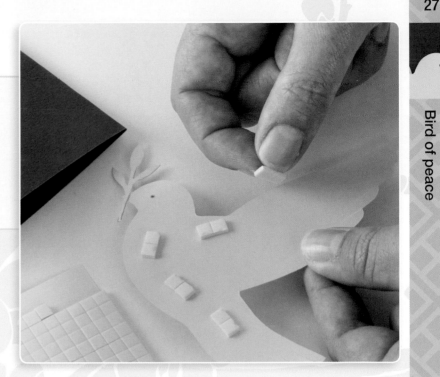

Tip

Omit the foam pads and glue the dove directly onto the card if you are posting it.

HEART GARLAND

Love is all you need! We hear this a lot, but do we really listen? And do we take time to love ourselves or are we always preoccupied with caring for others? Everyone needs to feel appreciated, and one way of doing this is to make something for yourself, perhaps as a reminder that you are loved. Try making this heart garland to hang at home, to remind yourself to focus on the important things in your life and on the people who really matter to you.

You will need
❀ Red, dark pink and light pink paper, 1cm (3⁄8in) wide ❀ Glue ❀ Scissors

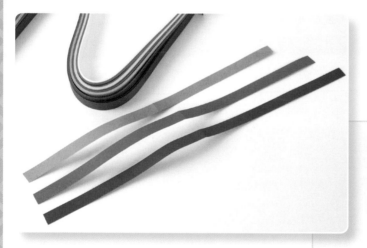

STEP 1

Cut the red paper into strips 29cm (11½in) long, the dark pink paper into strips 27cm (10⅝in) long, and the light pink paper into strips 25cm (10in) long.

STEP 2

Take a strip of each colour and place them together. Fold in half and glue the strips at the fold. With the light pink strip on the inside, glue one end of the three strips together. Repeat with the other end.

STEP 3

Bend the strips round to make a heart shape and glue the ends together. Remember to make sure the shortest length of paper is inside the heart shape.

STEP 4

Make more hearts in this way and glue the point of one heart to the top of another. Add more hearts to make a vertical garland.

Tip

This heart garland can be made from any type of paper – old sheet music is effective.

✂ ....
PROJECT 9

MOOD JOURNAL

It can be helpful to keep a regular account of your moods, thoughts and feelings. You may not find it easy to start with, but over time you will become comfortable with recording your high and low moods and the events which may have brought them about. When you notice a change in your mood, make a note of it and the circumstances, such as what you were doing and where and who you were with. You can easily fit this mood journal into a handbag and carry it with you. The silver outlines are a reminder of the old saying that 'every cloud has a silver lining'!

You will need
✽ Journal sized 11.5cm x 16.5cm (4½in x 6½in)
✽ Silver pen ✽ Rainbow-coloured paper
✽ Cocktail stick ✽ Glue ✽ Scissors ✽ Pencil

STEP 1
Use the templates on page 93 to draw cloud shapes on rainbow-coloured paper. Cut two large and two small clouds, or however many you need to cover your journal.

STEP 2
With a cocktail stick, apply a thin layer of glue to the paper shapes. Ensure that the glue reaches the edges of the shapes or they will lift off the journal. Arrange the clouds on the journal with the flat bases at the bottom.

STEP 3

Outline each cloud shape with a fine silver pen. You could use the silver pen to write the date or 'mood journal' on the cover.

Tip

Rainbow paper can be made using shaving cream and poster paints. Put the shaving cream in a tray, dot different coloured paints on top, swirl the colours with a cocktail stick and place your paper on top. Lift up the paper and scrape the shaving cream off.

✂ PROJECT 10

BAG OF SMILES

Giving is just the best feeling. If you have made the gift yourself or decorated the bag you give it in, this adds extra meaning. The creative act helps to lighten your mood and allows time for reflection. If a friend or family member is going through a rough time, we often feel powerless to help them. Sometimes the best way to reach the person is to give a thoughtful gift. It doesn't have to be large or expensive. A paper bag with a beaming sun radiating from it is quickly made and stands out from generic shop-bought bags.

You will need
❀ Brown gift bag, 9cm x10cm (3½in x 4in)
❀ Sheets of paper in orange and yellow
❀ Googly eyes, 3mm (⅛in) diameter
❀ Paper punch ❀ Black pen
❀ Pencil ❀ Ruler ❀ Scissors ❀ Glue

STEP 1
Using a pencil and ruler, mark the centre of the bag with a small circle.

STEP 2
Take the yellow and orange paper and cut narrow strips with large scissors. Angle the scissors so that the lengths are a long triangle shape. Start by gluing lengths of yellow paper to the bag, radiating out from the pencil mark. Build up the design by gluing on more strips of yellow and orange to complete the circle.

STEP 3
Using a paper punch, cut a circle of yellow paper 1.5cm (⅝in) in diameter. If you don't have a punch, draw round a coin and cut the circle by hand. Attach the googly eyes to the circle, draw on a smiling mouth and glue it onto the bag in the centre of the sunburst.

Tip
If you don't have googly eyes, just draw some eyes with black pen.

PROJECTS

2

Now you have gained confidence in papercrafting, have a go at these more advanced projects.

LOTUS FLOWER

The lotus flower is a beautiful symbol of healing, with significance reaching back to Ancient Egyptian times. It denotes creation and rebirth, as it grows from the depths of a muddy pool to emerge from the water's surface and burst into blossom. According to tradition, the muddier the water the more beautiful the flower. The lotus flower is useful in meditation, particularly for people who've had a tough time in their lives. In this project, the flower is made with sheets of plain white printer paper. It could be used as a table centrepiece for a special meal.

You will need
- ✿ Basic tool kit
- ✿ White paper A4
- ✿ Yellow paper
- ✿ Cocktail stick
- ✿ Green card
- ✿ Soft pencil
- ✿ Scissors
- ✿ Glue

STEP 1
Start by cutting three squares of white paper with the following dimensions: 9cm (3½in), 10cm (4in) and 12cm (4¾in). Fold each square in half and then half again. You should have three folded pieces.

STEP 2
Copy the three sizes of template on page 93. Draw around the petal shapes on each folded square of paper with a soft pencil. Ensure the template is positioned on the paper as shown, with its point at the folded corner.

STEP 3

With scissors, cut round the pencil lines on each of the three folded pieces. Make sure you cut just inside the pencil line, rather than on it. This way, no pencil marks will show on the final flower.

STEP 4

Open out each folded piece of paper. You now have three shapes, each with eight petals. Pinch the end of each petal and curl it upwards.

STEP 5

Now place the three layers on top of one another, with the largest at the base and the smallest on top. Stick them together by applying a small amount of glue to the centre of each shape. Stick the flower onto the green card.

STEP 6

For the flower centre, take a 40cm (15¾in) strip of yellow paper 1cm (⅜in) wide. With small scissors, cut halfway across the paper to make a 'fringe', leaving an uncut margin on the opposite side. Fringe the length for 10cm (4in) only.

STEP 7

Take a cocktail stick and wrap the yellow paper around this, starting at the unfringed end. Continue rolling the paper right to the fringed end and then glue in place. Remove the cocktail stick and glue the yellow shape to the centre of the flower, spreading out the fringed ends.

Tip

Lotus flowers can be made from coloured paper, such as light pink or green. If you don't have yellow paper, colour a strip of white paper with a yellow felt-tip pen.

Mood therapy
TEA LIGHT HOLDER

After a long, busy day, nothing beats sitting down in a comfortable armchair with your favourite hot drink. The contrasting moods of noisy/hectic and peace/calm relate to yin and yang and represent the balance we strive to achieve between the active and the relaxed aspects of our lives. As the yin-yang symbol suggests, when the two are together they help you attain that elusive goal – balance in your body and life. Keep this tea light holder as a visual reminder of yin and yang in your home, to maintain a positive and balanced frame of mind (see page 40 for instructions).

✂ PROJECT 12

YIN-YANG TEA LIGHT HOLDER

A well-known symbol of Taoism, yin-yang means completeness. Yin and yang are two equal halves that make a whole and show that everything in the universe consists of two opposing but complementary forces, for example, night and day, life and death, health and sickness. Each part is dependent on the other and is everchanging. The yin-yang symbol means balance, harmony and stability, and can be applied creatively. It is usually shown in black and white, but here I've used coloured card with a simple design cut in to let the light through.

You will need
❀ Basic tool kit ❀ Scrap card
❀ Sheets of card in blue, pink and orange
❀ Pearl decorations

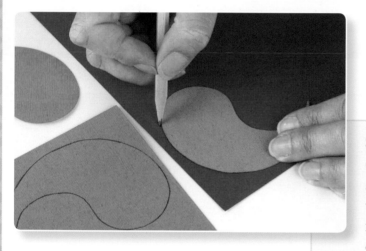

STEP 1
Copy the template on page 94 onto scrap card, such as a cereal packet, and cut out. Use this template to draw four shapes on pink card and four shapes on orange card. Use scissors to cut out all eight shapes.

STEP 2
In pencil, draw a simple design onto each shape; you can use the example as a guide or make your own. Place the shape on a cutting mat and, with a sharp craft knife, cut out the design you have just drawn. Do this for all eight shapes.

STEP 3

Now take a piece of blue card 13cm (5in) wide x 28cm (11in). Score three times across the card at a distance of 1cm (⅜in), 14cm (5½in) and 27cm (10⅝in) from one edge. Cut two circles 8cm (3⅛in) in diameter in each panel. Repeat with another piece of the same colour card.

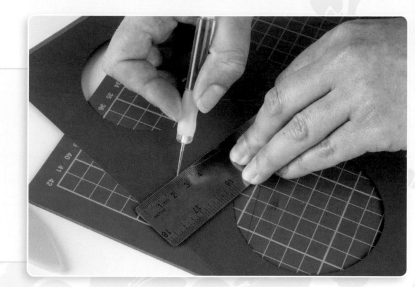

STEP 4

Apply a small amount of glue to an orange shape and carefully place a pink shape on top so that they overlap by 1mm (1/16in), making a circle. Glue the other pieces together so that you have four circles.

STEP 5

Now apply a small amount of glue around the edge of the circle and place it over the aperture in the blue card. Press firmly to make sure it is stuck in place. Glue the remaining three circles in place on the other apertures, ensuring that two are horizontal and two are vertical.

STEP 6

On one of the pieces of blue card, put a strip of double-sided sticky tape down both the short edges that were scored at 1cm (⅜in). Remove the backing tape and stick together to make a box. Press the card firmly to ensure it is stuck.

STEP 7

Finally, place small pearl decorations on each of the pink and orange shapes. If you don't have decorations, you could place a small circle of orange on the pink shape and vice versa.

Tip

Only use battery-operated tea lights with paper decorations such as this.

✂ PROJECT 13

BEACH COLLAGE

The beach is a place of relaxation and tranquillity. The combination of sun, sand and sea soothes the nerves and works wonders for our spirits. The fresh sea air seems to blow away worries and troubles. Unfortunately, most of us can't spend all our lives at the beach, so on dull days we have to visualize a sunny paradise. Visualization is a great way to relax the mind and body. This simple collage of mixed media can be hung near a work desk to help recapture the positive mood of happy, sunny days at the seaside.

You will need
❀ Picture frame, 12cm (4¾in) x 34cm (13¼in)
❀ Sheets of paper in a mix of blues, yellows and creams
❀ Beach ephemera ❀ Glue ❀ Scissors

STEP 1
Collect papers left over from other projects; choose a mixture of blues, yellows and creams. Gather together papers of different textures and weights with some handmade and tissue papers, if you have them. Tear into strips the width of your picture frame.

STEP 2
Start to arrange the collage by layering the papers. It is a good idea to lay them down and arrange them before gluing in place. Try to overlap contrasting paper textures. Start with the creams, moving on to yellow papers and then light blues.

STEP 3

Continue to layer the papers, working from light blues to darker blues. Here I've cut three fish from dark blue paper and put them under the layers. One fish is jumping.

STEP 4

In the frame, place a small selection of ephemera you have collected from the beach. I have used two shells and two pieces of beach glass at the bottom of the frame. I've glued a beach-hut image to the top of the collage.

Tip

Handmade paper has no grain and will tear more easily if slightly dampened along the tear line.

MANDALA DECORATION

A mandala is an evenly balanced circle pattern that represents wholeness, a symbol of the structure of life itself. Mandalas are used for meditation and have become popular images for mindfulness and relaxation. Here the mandala pattern is represented using paper pricking and stamping techniques.

You will need

❀ Sheets of card in purple, mauve, green and light green

❀ Music-patterned rubber stamp

❀ Green ink pad ❀ Small foam pads

❀ Pricking tool and mat ❀ Scissors

❀ Circle punches (optional) ❀ Glue

❀ Purple ribbon 7mm (²⁄₈in) wide

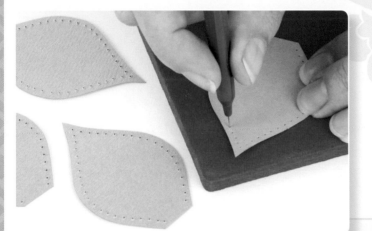

STEP 1

Using the template on page 94, cut six large leaves from green card. Place one leaf onto a pricking mat then, using a sharp, fine pricking tool, pierce the card around the edge to make a border of holes. The paper that is pushed through with the pricking creates a texture on the underside. Repeat for all the leaves.

STEP 2

Cut a circle of green card 4cm (1½in) in diameter and glue it onto the centre of an 18cm (7in) square of purple card. Now arrange the six leaves around the circle, ensuring that the textured side from the paper pricking is uppermost. Place a small foam pad on the tip of each leaf and apply glue to the base before fixing it in position.

STEP 3

Ink a music-patterned rubber stamp with green ink and stamp it onto light green card. Lift the rubber stamp, re-ink it and stamp it again to cover half the card.

STEP 4

Using the page 94 template, cut six small leaves from the stamped light green card, and six small leaves from the non-stamped light green card.

STEP 5

Attach a mauve circle to the centre of the card as a guide. Fix a small foam pad to the tip of each leaf and glue the patterned leaves around the circle. Arrange the plain smaller leaves around the outside, tucking them under the large leaves.

Tip

If you don't have a pricking tool, you can use a fine needle and a cork.

STEP 6

Finally, add a purple circle 2.5cm (1in) in diameter to the centre and glue a slightly smaller light green circle on top of this. The small green circle should also be paper pricked. Mount the purple card onto light mauve card that is 18.5cm (7¼in) square, then affix this to strong card or mountboard. Attach a 20cm (8in) length of purple ribbon in a loop to the reverse side.

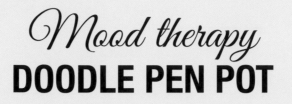

Mood therapy
DOODLE PEN POT

Doodling a few moments away with pen and paper is great mood therapy. It calms our thoughts and helps us to focus when stress levels are high. With no pressure to sketch a masterpiece, random squiggles and colouring can help to rest and quieten our minds. It can also work to stimulate new ideas and creativity. Try making and decorating a pen pot so that your doodling materials are always close at hand (see page 52 for instructions).

DOODLE POT

A doodle is a shape, pattern, scribble or word. Doodling can be an outlet for boredom or frustration – often the urge to doodle can be stronger the more our stress levels rise. For many people, doodling is a safety valve that allows pressure to be expressed in a creative way. You may have a book of plain paper that you doodle in on your daily commute. Here I've made a coloured doodle into a desk tidy as a reminder that it's fine and therapeutic to play with lines and colours!

You will need
❀ Cylindrical container
❀ Pink paper or thin card, 9cm (3½in) x 25cm (10in)
❀ Fine-tipped black pen ❀ Coloured felt-tip pens
❀ Ruler ❀ Double-sided tape ❀ Glue

STEP 1
For your pot, you could recycle a household food container, such as a cocoa or chocolate powder tin. Cut a strip of thin pink card or thick paper to fit around your empty container with a 1cm (⅜in) overlap. Here I've used a container 9.5cm (3¾in) high and 7.5cm (3in) in diameter.

STEP 2
With a fine black pen, draw a freestyle swirl all over the card. If the card is textured, make sure it is the non-textured side you are working on. To get the flow of the swirls, try a couple of practice runs doodling on scrap paper.

STEP 3
The swirls will have created different-sized areas that can be coloured in. With fine-tipped felt pens, colour in where the lines overlap. Here I've used just three colours of pen – orange, red and pink.

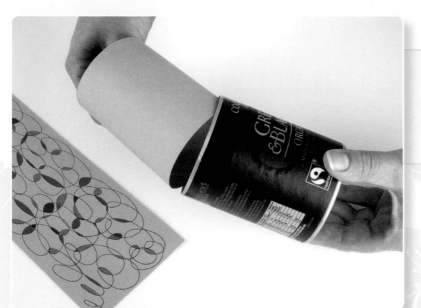

STEP 4

Now cut a piece of pink card for the inside of the container. Insert, and secure it in place with glue.

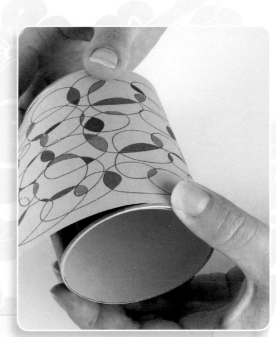

STEP 5

Place double-sided tape on the reverse side of the card you have doodled on, then wrap it round the pot and secure in place. Ensure the overlap is stuck down firmly, using glue if needed.

Tip

Watercolour pencils can be used instead of felt-tip pens.

✂ **PROJECT 16**

YLANG YLANG FLOWER

The ylang ylang flower is a tropical yellow bloom with a pretty swirling shape. Its essential oil is widely used in aromatherapy and perfumery. The delicate fragrance also has many benefits. In aromatherapy, the flower oil is used to dispel negative emotions, boost confidence and improve self-esteem. Here the paper flower can be used as a decoration to capture the uplifting properties of ylang ylang in your everyday life, to reduce stress and lift depression. The yellow flower tendrils are unusual and delicate, making it a wonderful decoration for home or work.

You will need
❀ Yellow handmade paper
❀ Green floristry wire
❀ Green floristry tape
❀ Cotton wool balls
❀ Green tissue paper
❀ Yellow tissue paper
❀ Strong green paper
❀ Green felt-tip pen
❀ Scissors
❀ Pencil

STEP 1
Take a cotton wool ball and pull a piece away to make a smaller ball about 1cm (⅜in) in diameter. Take a length of green floristry wire 30cm (12in) long and bend the top of the wire round the cotton ball to hold it in place. Twist this short end of wire around the main length of the wire.

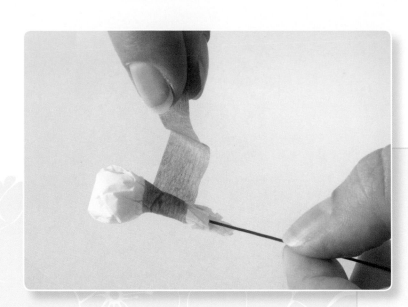

STEP 2

Cut a 3cm (1¼in) square of yellow tissue paper and use it to cover the ball. Wrap a length of green floristry tape around the wire to hold the paper in place. The tape will stick to itself.

STEP 3

Cut six long petals from the yellow handmade paper. Ensure the paper you are using is strong, or glue two sheets together to make a thicker piece. With a green felt-tip pen, colour the base of each petal.

STEP 4

Now glue a petal to the flower centre, ensuring that the green coloured base is fixed to the wire. Glue two more petals around the flower centre – they should cover the tissue. Now glue three more petals to overlap the first set. Wrap more floristry tape round the base of the petals to hold in place and continue wrapping the tape down the wire.

STEP 5

Bend the head of the flower over. Wrap the petal ends around the pencil to curl. Remove the pencil and use your fingers to shape each petal. Use the strong green paper to make a leaf and glue it to the wire stem. Make several flowers for an arrangement.

Tip

Handmade papers are great to use in projects such as this, as they have texture and patterns that you don't find in machine-made papers.

Ylang ylang flower

Mood therapy
DREAMCATCHER

As we spend much of our time at home, and a substantial amount of that time asleep, it is important to make the most of our dream possibilities. Having quiet 'me' time at the end of the day or perhaps at the start, before setting out on a long day ahead, is vital for our happiness and wellbeing. A pretty dreamcatcher in warm, soft, natural earth colours is easy to create. Hang it in a window and let the gentle movement of the feathers soothe your spirit (see page 60 for instructions).

✂ PROJECT 17

DREAMCATCHER

Every parent wants their child to have beautiful dreams. Here we take inspiration from the Native American charm known as a 'dreamcatcher'. Originating with the Ojibwe Nation, the dreamcatcher has many meanings and purposes. It filters out bad dreams, catching them in the web, and allows only sweet dreams to enter the mind. The morning sun burns off the bad dreams as it rises. Here we translate a dreamcatcher into papercraft to encourage ourselves to slow down and be inspired by beautiful customs and beliefs.

You will need

✽ Sheets of card in brown, turquoise, yellow, ochre and orange
✽ Sheets of paper in turquoise and brown
✽ Wire hoop, 15cm (6in) in diameter
✽ Brown embroidery thread and needle
✽ Brown ribbon ✽ Cocktail sticks
✽ Glue

STEP 1

Make paper beads by rolling strips of paper. Here, brown and turquoise beads are made from lengths of paper 30cm (12in) long. The brown strips are 2cm (¾in) wide at one end, but have been cut to taper to a point at the other end. The turquoise strips are 1cm (⅜in) wide, and taper to a point. Starting with the widest end, roll a turquoise strip around a cocktail stick. Once the strip has been rolled and the narrow end reached, place glue on the point and press it to the roll to secure the bead. Now slide the bead off the cocktail stick. Make five turquoise beads and four brown beads.

STEP 2

Now cut feather shapes of different sizes from brown, light brown, turquoise, orange and ochre coloured card. To create a fringe, carefully cut into the feather shape at an angle, to the centre line. Fringe the card all the way along each side.

STEP 3

Thread the needle with a 20cm (8in) length of brown embroidery thread. Thread this through the end of a feather, then add a bead of each colour and a smaller feather. Make three strands of beads and feathers in this way – you can vary the combinations a little if you like.

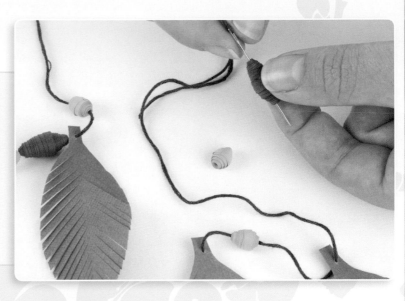

STEP 4

Tie each strand to the metal hoop, securing tightly.

STEP 5

Cut a circle of brown card 16cm (6¼in) in diameter and cut a 4cm (1½in) square hole in the centre. Now cut several 4cm (1½in) squares of card from turquoise, orange, yellow and ochre coloured card. Cut these in half diagonally to make triangles. Glue four yellow triangles to the brown circle.

STEP 6
Continue to build up the design by gluing on the triangles as shown.

Tip
If you don't have a metal hoop, you can use a circle of strong card, such as mountboard, to keep the dreamcatcher's shape.

STEP 7
Cut two turquoise triangles in half again and attach these four smaller triangles to the centre of the design. Tie a length of brown ribbon to the metal hoop and fix the brown circle to the hoop with strong glue.

✂ **PROJECT 18**

QUILLED FRIDGE MAGNETS

We may tell ourselves we can't afford hobbies, or don't have time for them, but not all hobbies cost money; many of them are economical, as they recycle items such as paper and card. The amount of time we allow for hobbies is within our control. Once the working day is over and the family chores completed, we can make time. Instead of flopping in front of the television and thinking we are relaxing, we might find it more satisfying to learn a new hobby. A craft such as paper quilling requires minimal tools, is cheap to do and produces lovely results.

You will need
❀ Quilling tool ❀ Quilling board
❀ Sheets of quilling paper 3mm (⅛in) wide in red, pink and mauve ❀ Thin card in purple and mauve
❀ Die cutter and scallop dies (optional)
❀ Large paper clips 10cm (4in) long
❀ Magnet ❀ Glue ❀ Scissors

STEP 1
Take a 40cm (15¾in) length of pink quilling paper and insert one end into the prongs of a quilling tool. Rotate the tool away from you with one hand, while maintaining a light tension on the paper with the other hand. Continue coiling with the quilling tool until the end of the paper is reached.

STEP 2
Remove the quilling tool from the coil. Place the coil onto the quilling board, circle size 2cm (¾in), to release and fill the circle. Then place a dot of glue on the end of the paper and press it to the coil, holding the circle shape. Make three pink and three mauve coils from 40cm (15¾in) lengths of quilling paper.

STEP 3

Remove the quilled shape from the board and pinch lightly with your fingers into a teardrop shape. Repeat for all the coils.

STEP 4

Make a scallop-edged circle from purple card with the die cutter tool and dies. Cut a smaller circle (2⅜in) in diameter from mauve card and glue it to the purple card. Glue three pink teardrop shapes, points inwards, to the mauve card. Then glue the three remaining shapes in between to form a flower. Make a loose closed coil from a 20cm (8in) length of pink quilling paper for the centre.

STEP 5

Turn over the card circle, glue the large paperclip to the reverse side with strong glue, and attach a magnet.

Tip

If you are new to this craft, practise making lots of coils to become familiar with the coiling and twirling.

ENVELOPES TO 'OPEN WHEN . . .'

If you are feeling low, write a goodbye letter to your symptoms, worries and negative thoughts. Then write words of encouragement and support to yourself. Self-acceptance is so important in our lives, as we are often our own harshest critics. Put these letters into envelopes in a box that is specially for you. Include envelopes to open when you need to smile; they can contain an image, photo, poem or message that makes you really happy. Then add an envelope containing a calm message to yourself to open when you are feeling angry. Continue the theme with envelopes to open when you are stressed or need encouragement. I decorated my envelopes with 'Washi tapes'. These originate in Japan and come in different colours, patterns and sizes. The tapes are easy to use and can be removed and replaced.

You will need
❀ Envelopes of assorted sizes in brown and pink
❀ Brown box 13cm (5in) square
❀ Washi tapes in pinks, purples and blues   ❀ Scissors

STEP 1
Pull out a length of Washi tape from the roll and stick it onto a pink envelope. Using a different pattern, place another strip above the first. Decorate the front and back of the envelope.

STEP 2
When decorating the envelope flap, use scissors to trim the excess tape; if you wrap the tape around the flap it will cover the gummed underside and you won't be able to seal the envelope.

STEP 3

Now decorate the brown box with the Washi tapes. Wrap lengths around the base, going all the way round. Then build up a grid pattern on the lid with lengths of tape.

STEP 4

Use different colours of Washi tape for different moods, according to the contents. The blues might be for when you want an envelope to open when you need calming down or are feeling blue. Cut a 'v' shape in the tapes for different effects.

Tip

Washi tapes can also be used to decorate cards or tags. You could use them in the gratitude jar project on page 22 to seal the paper strips.

Mood therapy
LAVENDER BOX

The fragrance of herbs and flowers has the power to evoke memories, feelings and warm positivity. Our sense of smell is directly linked to the emotional part of our brains, which is why the soft scent of lavender can have such a beneficial impact. The aroma can relax and soothe both mind and body and promote better sleep. Keep fresh scents and aromatic bath infusers in a pretty paper box, like this.

LAVENDER BOX

Lavender is pretty plant with delicate purple and mauve flowers; it is a favourite of many gardeners. A herb known for its calming and relaxing properties, it has historically been used for insomnia, anxiety, depression and natural stress relief. The scent of lavender can help you enter a deep sleep. It's important to unwind after a stressful day and making a papercraft item can help you do this. I used a quick scoring method to make this simple box for holding pot pourri, bath salts or fresh lavender.

You will need
* Scoring board and tool
* Card patterned on both sides, 30cm square (12in)
* Purple ribbon 6mm (¼in) wide
* Small hole punch

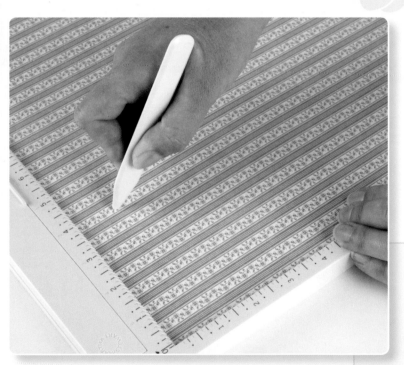

STEP 1

Take the square of patterned card. Choose which pattern will be inside the box (I've chosen the lined side). With this pattern face up, place the card on the scoring board. Using the pointed edge of the tool, score a line all the way down 10cm (4in) in from the left side. Then score a line 20cm (8in) in from the left side.

STEP 2

Turn the card 90 degrees and score lines again at 10cm (4in) and 20cm (8in) in from the left side. Lift the card from the scoring board and, using the flat side of the tool, fold it over at a score line and press down, making a good crease all the way along. Repeat this for all four score lines. Open out the card again.

STEP 3

Insert the corner piece into the scoring board. Place the paper floral side up against the corner piece. Score a line from the point of the corner piece down to the join of the score lines made in step 1. This score line will be 14cm (5½in) long. Score the other corner.

STEP 4
Push the corners inwards along the score lines to make the box shape, ensuring the floral pattern is on the outside and the line pattern is on the inside. The four points will meet in the centre of the box.

STEP 5
Punch a small hole in each point and thread purple ribbon through the holes. Tie the ribbon in a bow.

PROJECT 21

FAMILY ORGANIZER

Many people feel stressed when their lives are disorganized and out of control – when the house is a mess, for example, or when bills haven't been paid. This family organizer is made from card and clothes pegs covered in pretty paper. Reminders and notes can be pegged up in the kitchen so that they are visible and nothing gets forgotten! A chalk board could be added to the centre of the organizer for scribbling last-minute reminders.

You will need
- ❀ Two plates
- ❀ Cream mountboard
- ❀ Eight wooden clothes pegs
- ❀ Patterned paper ❀ Pencil
- ❀ Scissors ❀ Cutting mat
- ❀ Craft knife ❀ Glue

STEP 1

Using a plate as a guide, draw a circle 22cm (8½in) in diameter onto cream mountboard. Cut out this circle and then draw a central circle 8cm (3⅛in) in diameter. Place it on a cutting mat and, using a sharp craft knife, cut out this inner circle.

STEP 2

Use a larger plate 28cm (11in) in diameter to draw around on the reverse side of the patterned paper. Cut out the circle using large scissors.

STEP 3

Glue the mountboard circle to the reverse side of the patterned paper circle. Spray Mount can be used for an even coating of glue, but ensure that there is good ventilation in the room if you are using this or, better still, spray it outside.

STEP 4

Place the circle, patterned side down, on a cutting mat. With a craft knife, cut the wrapping paper in the inner circle of the mountboard. Make cuts starting at the edge of the mountboard to the very centre. Cut all the way round the circle.

STEP 5

Carefully fold over these triangles and glue them to the reverse side of the mountboard. Cut the outer edges of the paper, fold over and glue. Cover the reverse side with another mountboard circle.

STEP 6

Cut thin strips of the patterned paper and glue them to the clothes pegs. Eight pegs are used here, but you can add more if you wish.

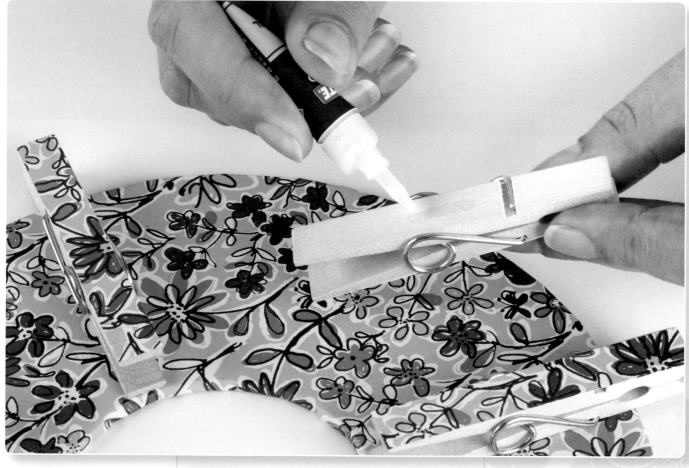

STEP 7

Use strong glue to secure the non-decorated side of the pegs to the circle. Make sure the holding end of the peg faces outwards. Position four pegs almost touching the inner circle and four more further out.

Tip

This organizer could be made with seven pegs, one for each day of the week.

Mood therapy
DOT FLOWER PICTURE

It is good for our wellbeing to have in our homes pictures that are pleasing to look at and make us smile or dream of faraway places. A picture we have created ourselves instils a sense of pride and achievement. It can be on display as a reminder of our innate abilities. It is ideal if both our subject and the creative process are serene and provide relaxation for the busy mind. The gentle focus required to produce a paper dot flower picture is perfect papercraft therapy (see page 80 for instructions).

✂ PROJECT 22

DOT FLOWER PICTURE

The earthy tones and flower image of this picture are inspired by the dot paintings of indigenous Australian art. The circles are made with a humble office hole punch and card, then each one is glued to the background card. The circles are arranged to 'enclose' dots within other dots, in this case as the petals of a flower. The land is the focus of much indigenous Australian art, and the use of warm hues and natural tones here evokes a sense of earthiness. This is a time-consuming project, but it can be built up over time in several sessions. The background could even be filled in with more dots.

You will need
❀ White picture frame, 25.5cm (10in) square and 4.5cm (1¾in) deep
❀ Sheets of card 23cm (9in) square in ochre, white, blue and pink
❀ Office hole punch which makes circles of 6mm (¼in) in diameter
❀ Pencil ❀ Cocktail stick
❀ Glue ❀ Tweezers

STEP 1
First take the base off the hole punch. Punch out dots in pink, blue and white card.

STEP 2

On a sheet of ochre coloured card 23cm (9in) square, lightly sketch a flower outline of five petals in pencil. With a cocktail stick, apply a small amount of glue to a pink circle and fix it to the flower outline. Continue to glue pink circles all round the flower outline, making sure they are evenly spaced. Then glue a row of blue dots inside the pink shape. Use tweezers to help position the circles.

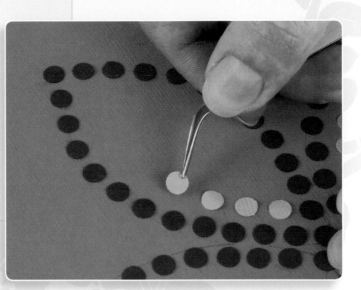

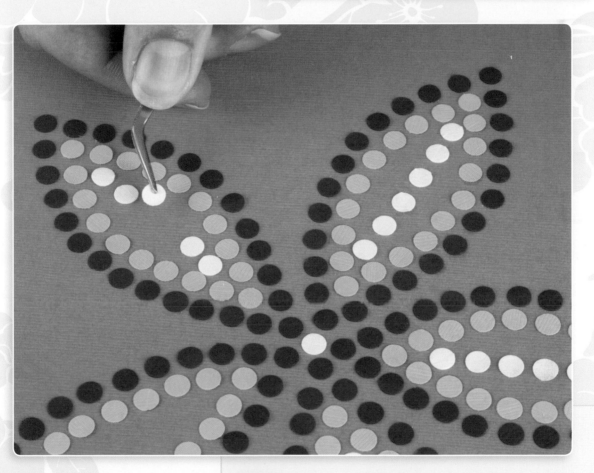

STEP 3

Once the rows of blue circles are complete, glue a white dot at each end of the inner petal. You want to make a straight line of white dots. For even spacing, work from each end to the centre. Do this for all five petals. Place a white dot in the centre of the flower.

STEP 4

Now remove the glass from the picture frame and insert the card. Reassemble the frame, without the glass, and secure the back. You can sign and date this artwork or add an envelope with your thoughts and feelings, to be opened at a later date.

 Tip

Instead of a flower, you could use dots to create random patterns, like a doodle.

BIRDS OF FREEDOM DOOR HANGER

It's time to escape to papercrafting paradise! Put a sign on the door of your room telling everyone you are having 'me' time and must not be disturbed. Put on some soothing music, empty your mind of the daily buzz, take a deep breath, relax, and focus on creating. For many of us, birds represent freedom and escape. The ability to enjoy the limitless space of the air is an ancient symbol of liberation. Perhaps we should all stop and listen to the inner free spirit in us, the voice of the birds, and develop our spiritual selves.

You will need

❀ Sheets of card in turquoise, red and light blue ❀ Scrap card and paper ❀ Foam mat ❀ Black beads ❀ Small blue beads ❀ Blue ink pad ❀ Sponge ❀ Needle and blue embroidery thread ❀ Flower punch ❀ Sticky tape ❀ Scissors

STEP 1

Take a sheet of red card and make ten flowers using the flower punch. Now punch a flower shape from scrap card to use as a stencil. Cut the hanger from turquoise card using the template on page 94. Dab the blue ink pad with a small piece of clean, dry sponge. Place the flower stencil on the card and press the sponge on the stencil to make a print. Continue to stencil flowers onto the hanger as shown in the photograph.

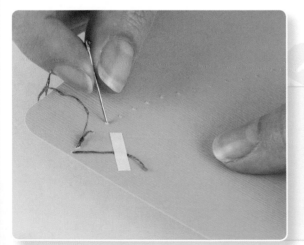

STEP 2

Place the hanger on a foam mat and, using the needle, prick holes to make a wavy line down its length. This is where the stitched line will be. Thread the needle with blue embroidery thread and secure the thread on the reverse side of the card with tape. Stitch along the wavy line, using backstitch.

STEP 3

Continue to stitch along the hanger with backstitch. If you need more thread, tape the ends on the reverse side. Don't use knots as these will pull through the card.

STEP 4

Cut two bird shapes and two wings from light blue card using the templates on page 95. Place these shapes on scrap paper and, with the sponge and blue ink, dab around the cutouts. Just colour the edges of the birds and wings lightly with ink.

STEP 5

Prick a hole in the centre of the red flowers then, with a needle and thread, attach a small blue bead to each, tying the thread in a knot on the reverse side. Sew or glue two black beads to the birds for eyes.

STEP 6

Glue the birds, their wings and the red flowers to the door hanger. Cut a second door hanger shape from turquoise card to cover the back of the stitching and to make the hanger more robust. Attach this to the stitched door hanger. You could add a message such as 'do not disturb' on the front.

Tip

If you find stitching paper tricky, then just use a blue pen to draw a stitched line.

Mood therapy
HAMSA HAND

When tired, we frequently lose perspective and become negative, but a few moments of focused time in solitude can revive our positivity. Drawing, colouring and doodling at home in the study, kitchen or living room after a difficult day can help us to gather our thoughts and refresh our spirits. The simplicity of black pen and white paper keeps it plain and pure, but your work can be as intricate as you wish (see page 90 for instructions).

HAMSA HAND PICTURE

The hamsa hand is a protective sign. It brings its owner happiness, health and good fortune. The hamsa hand often includes an eye symbol, which is thought to defend against the evil eye. An image that oversees our work desk can remind us that our families and loved ones will provide protection and are there for us. This hamsa hand outline is filled in with abstract marks. A mark can be a dot, a line, a swirl – anything you like – and can be loose and random or controlled and neat. There is no right or wrong; just feel free to make the marks you want.

You will need

❀ White picture frame 20cm (8in) square x 2.5cm (1in) deep
❀ Fine-tipped black pen
❀ Sheets of card in blue and white
❀ Foam board
❀ Soft pencil ❀ Scissors
❀ Glue

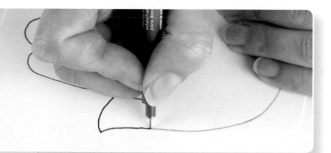

STEP 1

Using a soft pencil and the template on page 95, draw the outline of the hamsa hand on white card 15cm (5⅞in) square. Carefully go over this outline with the fine-tipped black pen. Don't worry if your outline isn't perfect, it will become incorporated into the design later on.

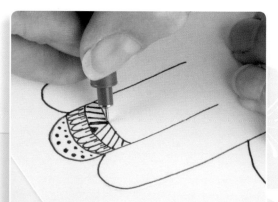

STEP 2

With the black pen, start drawing patterns on the fingertips. Starting with a small area means you can build and develop as you relax and feel more confident.

STEP 3

Continue to make marks by drawing lines, dots and other patterns. Draw an eye shape in the palm area of the hand, then work outwards from this, filling the area. Try to make some areas lighter than others to vary the density of the design.

STEP 4

When the hand is complete, mount the white card onto foam board 14cm (5½in) square. Cut the blue card to 18cm (7in) square, fit it into the picture frame and attach the foam board to this.

 Tip

You could make this into a true Zentangle piece by using tangles and designs from that craft.

TEMPLATES

Project 3
Take heart!

Project 4
Tree of life

Project 7
Bird of peace

Project 9
Mood journal

Project 11
Lotus flower

94

Templates

Project 12
Yin-yang tea light holder

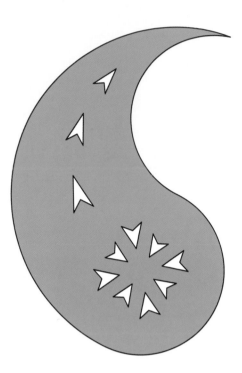

Project 14
Mandala decoration

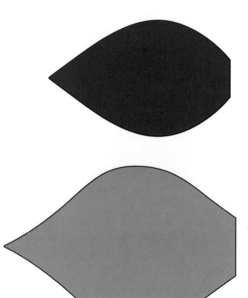

Project 23
Birds of freedom door hanger

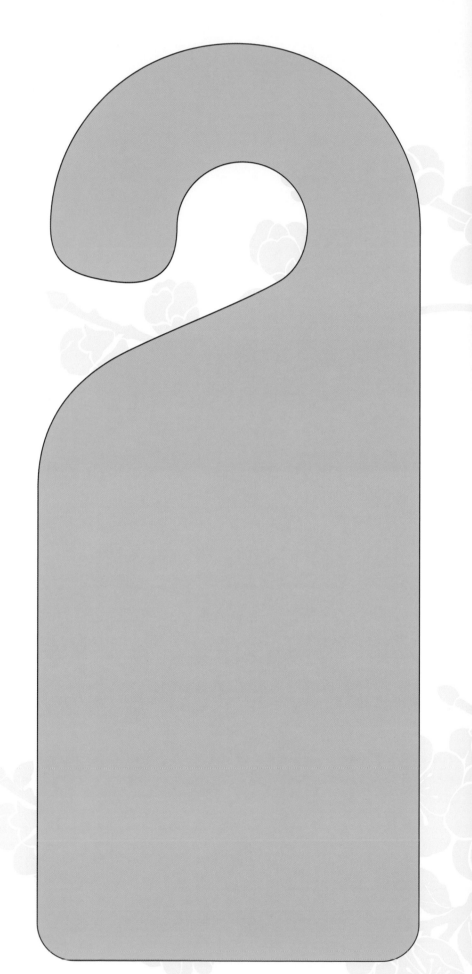

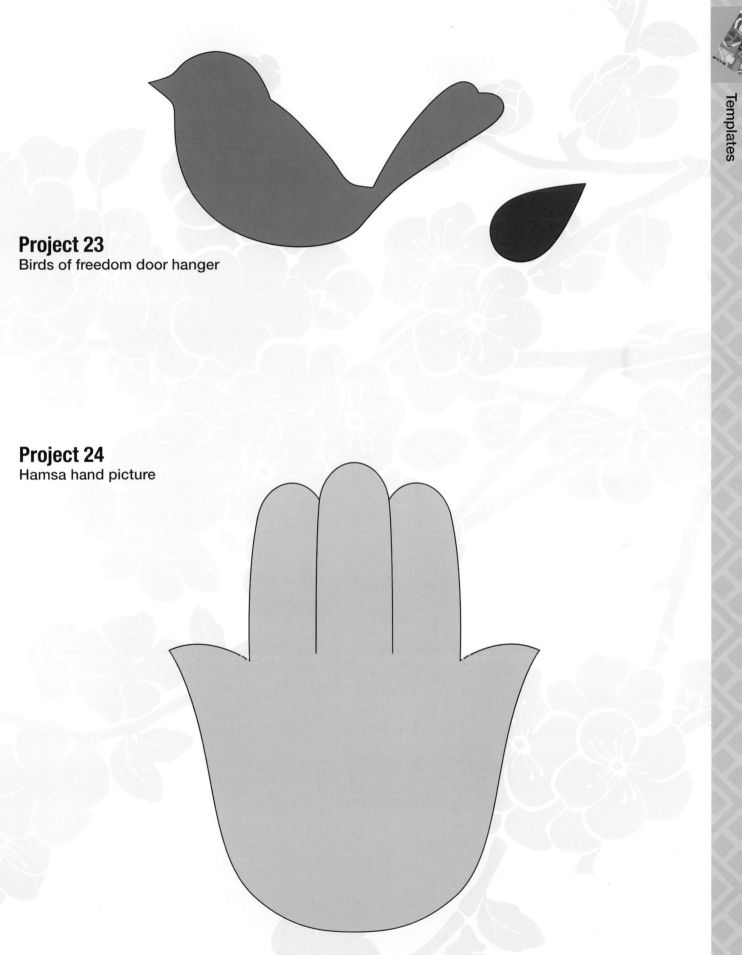

Project 23
Birds of freedom door hanger

Project 24
Hamsa hand picture

ACKNOWLEDGMENTS

I would like to thank the team at Arcturus for giving me the opportunity to indulge my passion for papercrafts in creating this fabulous book. Many thanks to Karl Adamson for all the photography, helping to make everything clear and easy to follow and creating the styled shots. Thank you to Diane Boden of JJ Quilling Design for the quality paper strips and tools used in the quilling project. Many thanks to Sizzix for creating the wonderful Big Shot die cutting tool that allows us crafters to make papercrafts using the huge array of die cut templates.

I would also like to thank Paperchase for the wonderful gift wrap with such great designs; Martha Stewart Crafts for excellent tools, such as the scoring board; Graphic 45 for their pretty scrapbooking papers; and We R Memory Keepers for fab Washi tapes. And, finally, thanks to Fiskars for great cutting tools and Letraset for professional pens, all essential in the making of this book.